Media Literacy for Kids

Learning About
Plagiarism

by Nikki Bruno Clapper

Consultant: JoAnne DeLurey Reed
Librarian and Teacher

CAPSTONE PRESS
a capstone imprint

Pebble Plus is published by Capstone Press,
1710 Roe Crest Drive, North Mankato, Minnesota 56003
www.capstonepub.com

Library of Contress Cataloging-in-Publication Data
Clapper, Nikki Bruno, author.
  Learning about plagiarism / by Nikki Bruno Clapper.
    pages cm. — (Pebble plus. Media literacy)
  Summary: "Introduces readers to the media literacy skills needed to understand plagiarism.
Includes a hands-on activity related to media literacy"— Provided by publisher.
  Audience: Ages 4-8
  Audience: K to grade 3
  ISBN 978-1-4914-6049-8 (library binding)
  ISBN 978-1-4914-6069-6 (ebook pdf)
1. Plagiarism--Juvenile literature. 2. Literary ethics--Juvenile literature. 3. Media literacy--Juvenile literature.
I. Title. II. Series: Pebble plus. Media literacy for kids.
PN167.C56 2016
808.02'5--dc23 2015006646

Editorial Credits
Gillia Olson, editor; Cynthia Della-Rovere, designer; Wanda Winch, media researcher;
Laura Manthe, media specialist

Photo Credits
All images by Capstone Studio: Karon Dubke except: Shutterstock: Multiart, cover (left), racom, 9

Note to Parents and Teachers

The Media Literacy for Kids set supports Common Core State Standards related to language
arts. This book describes and illustrates plagiarism. The images support early readers in
understanding the text. The repetition of words and phrases helps early readers learn new
words. This book also introduces early readers to subject-specific vocabulary words, which
are defined in the Glossary section. Early readers may need assistance to read some words
and to use the Table of Contents, Glossary, Read More, Internet Sites, Critical Thinking Using
the Common Core, and Index sections of the book.

Printed in the United States of America in North Mankato, Minnesota.
122015   009362R

Table of Contents

What Is Plagiarism?

Plagiarism means using someone else's words, pictures, or ideas as if they were yours. Plagiarism is a form of stealing.

People often learn by copying each other. It can be fun. But plagiarism is a bad type of copying.

Imagine that you write a poem. Your friend enters your poem in a competition and says it is his. He wins a prize. How do you feel?

Winner
My Poem

Give and Take Credit

Your friend plagiarized. He did not give you credit for your work. When you write a poem, you own it. You are the author.

All authors deserve credit.

Giving credit is a sign

of respect. You say,

"This person had a great idea.

I want to share it."

Use Sources the Right Way

An author's work is called
a source. Sources can be such
things as poems, drawings,
websites, or videos. Sources
help you write research reports.

You must always cite your sources, and give credit to the authors. If you do not cite your sources, you are plagiarizing.

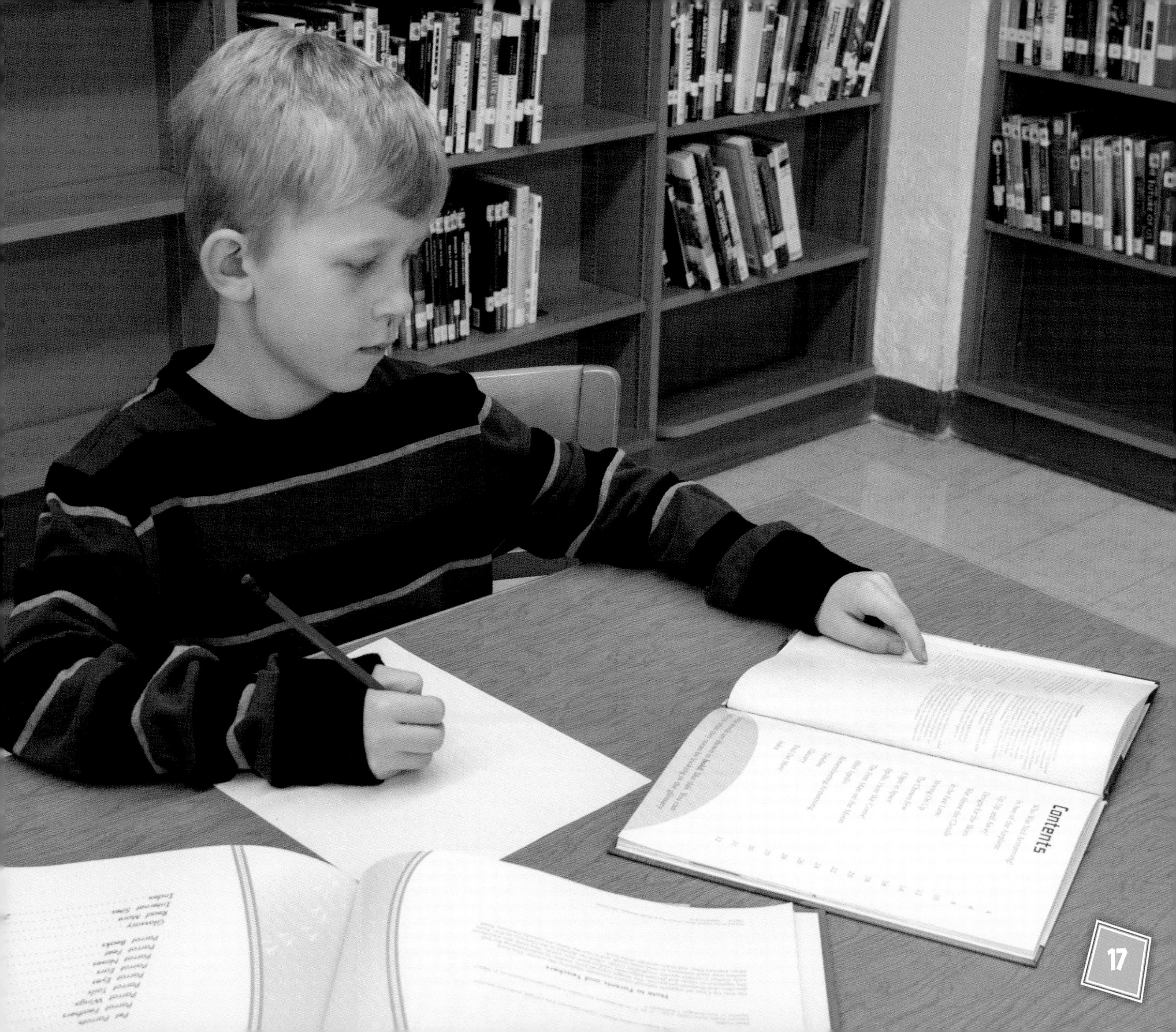
Contents

When you use a source, describe the author's ideas in your own words. If you use his or her exact words, put them in quotation marks (" ").

Great ideas are everywhere.

Some of them are yours!

Now you know how to share

ideas without plagiarizing.

Activity: A Story in Your Words

Practice using your own words by doing this fun activity.

1. Read a story that you like.

2. On a piece of paper, rewrite the story in your own words. Do not change the meaning of the story. Just retell it in mostly different words. Now you have two versions of the story.

3. Next, ask a friend to read the story too. Do not show your version of the story to your friend. Then give your friend a blank piece of paper and a pencil. Ask your friend to rewrite the story in his or her own words. Now you have three versions of the story.

4. Swap pieces of paper with your friend. Read each other's version of the story.

What You Need

2 pieces of paper

2 pencils

1 friend

5. Talk about these questions with your friend:

What was it like to rewrite the story? Was it easy? Was it hard?

Which retelling is most like the original story?

Which retelling is least like the original story?

Who is the author of the story? Why?

Glossary

author—a person who creates a work of art

cite—to give proper credit for the work of another person

credit—recognition of an author

describe—to tell about something in words

deserve—to be worthy of something because you earned it

plagiarism—copying someone else's work and passing it off as your own

plagiarize—to copy someone else's work and pass it off as your own

research—studies about a subject

respect—belief in the quality and worth of something or someone

source—someone or something that provides information

version—a telling of something from a certain point of view

Read More

Fox, Kathleen. *The Pirates of Plagiarism.* Janesville, Wis.: Upstart Books, 2010.

Manushkin, Fran. *Stick to the Facts, Katie: Writing a Research Paper with Katie Woo.* Katie Woo, Star Writer. North Mankato, Minn.: Picture Window Books, 2014.

Internet Sites

FactHound offers a safe, fun way to find Internet sites related to this book. All of the sites on FactHound have been researched by our staff.

Here's all you do:

Visit *www.facthound.com*

Type in this code: 9781491460498

 Check out projects, games and lots more at **www.capstonekids.com**

23

Critical Thinking Using the Common Core

1. What are some examples of sources? (Key Ideas and Details)

2. Describe a time when someone copied you but it was not plagiarism. (Integration of Knowledge and Ideas)

Index

Word Count: 215
Grade: 1
Early-Intervention Level: 20